CD INCLUDED

HAL•LEONARD
BIG BAND
PLAY-ALONG
VOLUME 3

GUITAR

Duke Ellington

TITLE	PAGE	CD TRACK
Caravan	2	1
Chelsea Bridge	4	2
Cotton Tail	6	3
I'm Beginning to See the Light	10	4
I'm Just a Lucky So and So	12	5
In a Mellow Tone	14	6
In a Sentimental Mood	16	7
Mood Indigo	18	8
Satin Doll	20	9
Take the "A" Train	22	10
B♭ Tuning Notes		11

ISBN: 978-1-4234-4980-5

HAL•LEONARD®
CORPORATION
7777 W. BLUEMOUND RD. P.O. BOX 13819 MILWAUKEE, WI 53213

T0056187

Visit Hal Leonard Online at
www.halleonard.com

CARAVAN

Words and Music by DUKE ELLINGTON,
IRVING MILLS and JUAN TIZOL
Arranged by MICHAEL SWEENEY

GUITAR

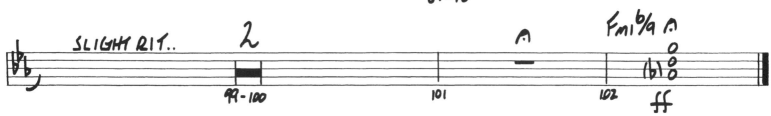

CHELSEA BRIDGE

Guitar

By BILLY STRAYHORN
Arranged by MARK TAYLOR

COTTON TAIL

Guitar

By DUKE ELLINGTON
Arranged by MARK TAYLOR

GUITAR

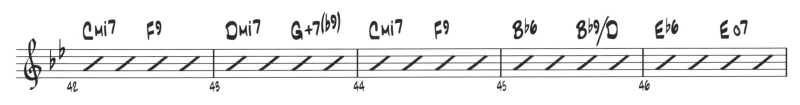

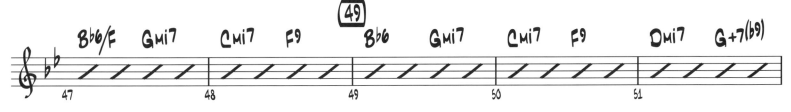

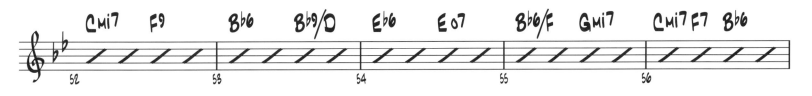

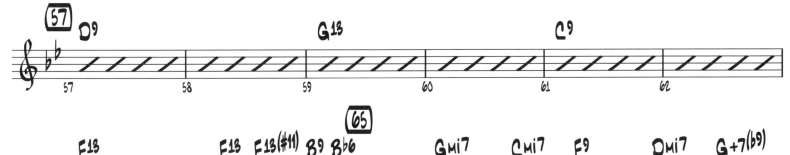

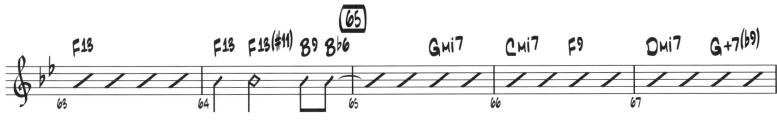

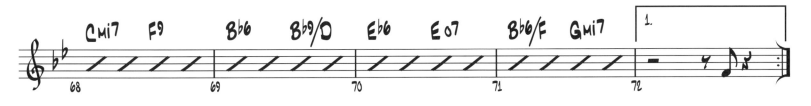

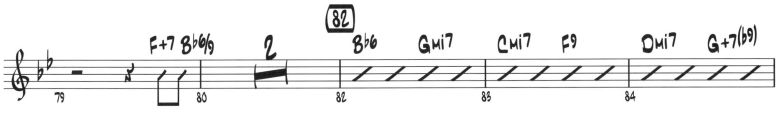

GUITAR

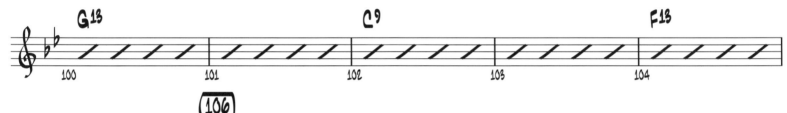

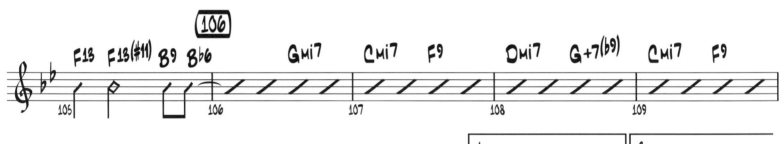

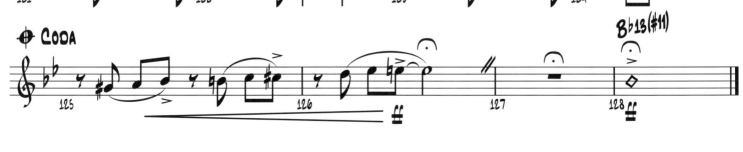

THIS PAGE HAS BEEN LEFT BLANK TO ACCOMMODATE PAGE TURNS.

Featured in SOPHISTICATED LADIES

I'M BEGINNING TO SEE THE LIGHT

Words and Music by DON GEORGE, JOHNNY HODGES,
DUKE ELLINGTON and HARRY JAMES
Arranged by MARK TAYLOR

Guitar

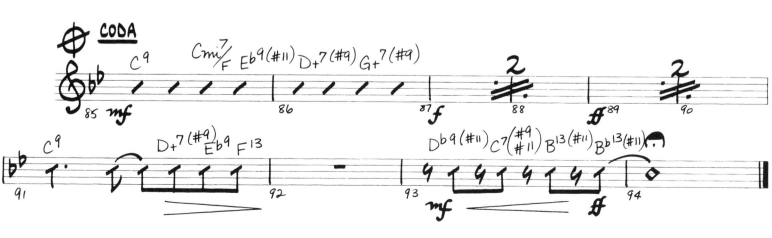

I'M JUST A LUCKY SO AND SO

Words by MACK DAVID
Music by DUKE ELLINGTON
Arranged by ROGER HOLMES

Guitar

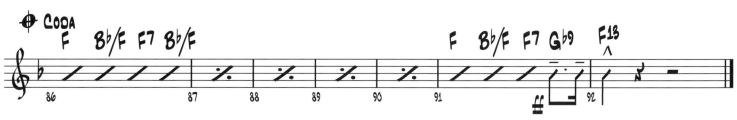

IN A MELLOW TONE

Guitar

By Duke Ellington
Arranged by MARK TAYLOR

GUITAR

Bb7   Eb7   Bbmi7 A13   Ab6   Fmi7 E7(b9)

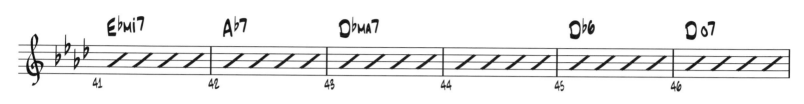

Ebmi7   Ab7   DbMA7   Db6   Do7

Ab6/Eb   F9   F+7(b9)   Bb9   Eb7

Eb9 D9 Eb9   E9 F9 53 Bb9   Eb9 D9 Eb9   Bbmi7 Eb9   Ab6

(Ab6)   Fmi7 Emi9   Ebmi9   Ab7   DbMA7

(DbMA7)   Db6   Do7   Ab6/Eb   F9   Bb9

Eb9sus   Eb9 Eb7(b9) Ab6   Eb7   F9 69 Bb7   Eb7

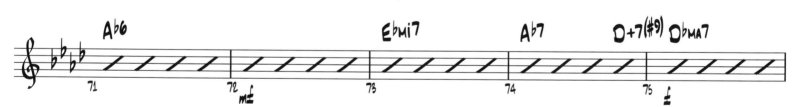

Ab6   Ebmi7   Ab7   D+7(#9) DbMA7

(DbMA7)   Ab13 Db6   Do7   Ab6/Eb   F9   Gb9 F13

B13 Bb13 Ab13 F13 E9   Eb9 Bb9 A+9 Ab6   Ab13(#11)

IN A SENTIMENTAL MOOD

Guitar

By Duke Ellington
Arranged by MARK TAYLOR

GUITAR

Mood Indigo

Guitar

Words and Music by DUKE ELLINGTON,
IRVING MILLS and ALBANY BIGARD
Arranged by JOHN BERRY

GUITAR

SATIN DOLL

By Duke Ellington
Arranged by MARK TAYLOR

Guitar

GUITAR

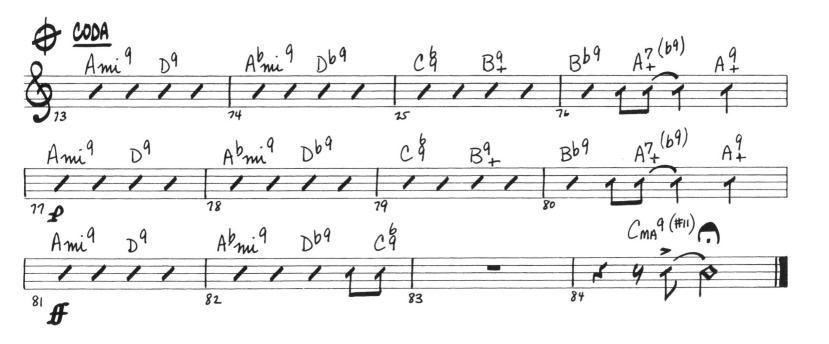

TAKE THE "A" TRAIN

Words and Music by
BILLY STRAYHORN
Arranged by DAVE BARDUHN

Guitar

GUITAR